Raul Moat – Britain's Biggest Police Manhunt

ISBN: 9798784132482

Disclaimer: The author nor the book
accept any responsibility for
inaccuracies the book content was
researched in depth and whilst every
effort has been taken the author can
reply only on the quality if research
materials available.

Table of Contents

CHAPTER ONE

Britain's biggest manhunt

In 2010 the largest manhunt in modern British history was launched when Raoul Moat declared war on Northumbria Police. For somebody to actively hunt a police officer almost unheard of. In just one week the 37-year-old ex con murdered and maimed in a vengeful rampage alone for seven days evading capture.

The former Newcastle bouncer evaded over 500 officers with no idea of where he was, and this man sent a wave of terror through rural Northumberland.

There was really only one way that it was going to end, but what caused this father of three to snap and embark on a deadly killing spree?

The 3rd of July 2010 Newcastle upon Tyne England a city known for its industrial past and vibrant Night Life.

Over the years Newcastle built up quite a reputation as a party city, incredibly popular with stag do's and Hen do's, a very vibrant nightlife that got a reputation as being a very friendly place.

It's a sort of city where you will run into the same people in the same pubs and clubs, crime is
never at zero anywhere you're
from, but Newcastle was, and still is a safe area to live, so what we saw in July 2010 was unexpected.

Where the normal for this area as Friday

night became Saturday

Morning, where revellers filled

Newcastle's clubs and bars, were

unaware that just 7 miles away one

party was about to come to a tragic end.

CHAPTER TWO

Who was Raoul Moat?

The gunman grew up in the Fenham area of Newcastle with his half-brother Angus. The brothers spent most of their childhood being raised by their grandmother.

Moat never knew his real father, who would later be revealed to be Peter Blake (below) from Birmingham.

Peter said he had no idea Moat's mum, Josephine Healey, had been pregnant when they separated.

And friends and family of the killer have said it could have been Moat's desperation to create the perfect family life he never had, that led to his violent rampage when he lost it all.

His best friend, Tony Ladler, was quoted to say, said: *"He just wanted a family life. He was with the kids all the time. When he was self-employed, he used to try and arrange all his work around the kids. He was really and speaking in the days after his friend's death Tony said he believed Moat had been unfairly harassed by police during his time as a doorman, and that this was something that contributed to his desperation".*

"We were both getting harassed off the police," he said. *"But it started to really get to him. He always used to rub his face when he got stressed and whenever*

I went round, he was sitting on the sofa rubbing his face.

"We have knocked around together since I was about three. He was just a normal lad, a proper lad who was into motorbikes and stuff and we were always out catching frogs and whatever. He was brought up by his gran and he only saw his mam when she came with presents every other Christmas."

Moat quit his job as a bouncer six years before the shootings and started his tree surgery business, Mr Trimmit.

But Tony claimed he still had regular run-ins with police.

Moat's shooting spree began two days after he was released from Durham Prison, where he served an 18-week sentence for assaulting a child. While Moat was in the run Angus spoke exclusively to a Newcastle newspaper about Moat.

He said he believed his younger brother had suffered a breakdown when he carried out the shootings.

And Angus argued Moat was not the Terminator-style killer he had been portrayed as during the manhunt, but simply a dad who wanted to keep his family together.

"I think Raoul had a lot of baggage to do with our family," he explained. "I think he just wanted a stable family life, but it has never worked and that he has had a breakdown".

"He came from a fairly dysfunctional background with very little maternal affection there, perhaps that's the reason why he was so desperate to form a stable family unit himself in adult life"

"When that has gone wrong perhaps it was the straw that broke the camel's back"

Growing up together in Newcastle's West End, Angus and his brother were virtually inseparable, despite their troubled family set-up Angus said his brother was always an outgoing fun-loving lad with lots of friends.

"My grandmother was the stabilising influence in our lives," said Angus.

"But both myself and Raoul took it in our stride. He was very outdoorsy. He liked to go out and play and he liked wildlife. There was nothing out of the ordinary about him."

As the brothers reached their early 20s, they grew apart. Moat became obsessed with weight training and started to spend most of his time with other bodybuilders, while Angus was more academic and went to university.

"Body-building was his thing," said Angus. "He trained every day and took a lot of pride in it."

And Angus said it was possible Moat had become hooked on steroids and these altered his state of mind.

"He was not a monster he was a normal loving guy. I know what he's done is horrific and if he wasn't my brother, I would be thinking the same as everyone else.

"But it's so hard for me to put the two people together in my mind. He was a friendly, generous soul, a very loyal individual, warm, with a great sense of humour, just a lovely, lovely guy.

"He was sensitive - perhaps too sensitive, which might have been what led him down this dark path. Perhaps he suffered one too many slights, one too many prangs, one too many buttons pressed."

Moat is said to have told police negotiators in Rothbury that he had no father, and that nobody cared for him.

Unbeknown to him, his real father Peter, who was living in Surrey at the time, had been desperate to speak to him.

Peter, who never met Moat, discovered it was his son at the centre of the manhunt through news coverage, and he has since said he blames himself for the tragedy.

In September 2010 he appeared on ITV's this morning programme and said: "If I'd have been there for him any time in his life, I think none of this would have happened, you would never have heard of him. "It's an incredible tragedy and I would like to say I'm sorry.

"I'm sorry not for what I did, but for what I didn't do. I'm dreadfully sorry to all the victims."

CHAPTER THREE

Durham Jail

Durham prison 2010 incarcerated among the gangsters, murderer's rapists and robbers was a mountain of

bodybuilder and nightclub doorman 37-year-old Moat was coming towards the end of an 18-week sentence for battering a young child.

but Moat a father of five claimed it was he who was the victim of continual police harassment.

In his mind he was certainly being victimised don't think it was an official police policy to harass him, but I think it's important in grievances which might be built inside him, he had this burning hatred of the police, and nothing could change his

mind or hi his Feelings. He had been arrested 12 times over the

last 10 years isn't I guess, but he

was also known for domestic abuse of former partners.

These domestic incidents where the police were involved often were passed to social services, but he saw himself as being persecuted by the social

services, and let's face it the states of social services in the UK, who knows it could be true.

He recorded hours of conversations with social services officials which he believed highlighted how they were trying to destroy his life.

After several domestic incidents social workers considered him to pose an unpredictable and violent threat, even more so after his conviction for assault on a child, this was the first time he'd been banged up but while he was inside it seemed those around him took their chance to break free from his controlling influence.

Highlighted in the book 'Operations Sayers' by Steve Wraith is the fact that Raoul had a letter passed in jail to Newcastle's notorious Stephen Sayers asking him for advice. Stephen decided to sleep on the matter before responding, but as it turned Moat was being released the following morning.

He wasn't getting hid kids

back, and these kids he claimed meant everything to him, his

home was being taken away, so he didn't have a home he's lost his business and he was being as being locked up. It was almost the perfect storm he felt his world was collapsing around him then Samantha Stobart his partner of six years and mother of one of his children broke up with him

CHAPTER FOUR

First Blood

02:30 AM In Birtley, near Gateshead the sound of gunfire was about to ring out through the quite residential streets. Following a night out in a local bar Samantha Stobart and Christopher Brown visited a friend's house, Samantha, and new boyfriend Christopher we're enjoying a social evening with her parents and friends.

Samantha Stobart in happier days with Raoul Moat

The young couple were unaware that an armed man with deadly intent was hiding in wait outside, just underneath the window.

As their evening ended Samantha and Christopher prepared to leave, they were a little nervous as Samantha's ex-boyfriend had just been released from prison

and they half expected trouble, Chris
had even asked the host
 if he could lend him a baseball bat, and
when didn't he took a weights bar out
with him instead. A little like to adage
"you don't take a gun to a Kinfe fight"

Christopher Brown

When both Samantha and Christopher emerged from the house, he confronted them he immediately shot Christopher in the upper body, and it is Christopher tried to runaway shot my second time while I was lying injured, he and reloaded the gun and shot a defenceless injured Christopher on the ground the third shot proved to be fatal then he attention to Samantha who was but this time inside the house and, he fired a shot through the window and then he calmly walked away?

One was left dead, another critically injured.

CHAPTER FIVE

Reactions

As Police slowly started releasing details they described it as a domestic disturbance, but local people at the scene were telling everyone that a man had been released from prison and came to the house and shot his shot his ex-girlfriend and shot her new partner.

As the morning wore on the name Raoul Moat was mentioned more and more, Raoul Thomas Moat, born on June the 17th 1973 by all accounts a man with an unstable childhood that was always looking for his dad.

From being young and his mum would never actually say who he was so he would elect father figures as standard normal family life his early years were further complicated by his mother's mental health issues, she was never there and Raoul was mainly living with his Granma.

She gave him a good quality of life and looked after him and he idolised her. He was in a happy zone until his mother remarried in 1986 when he went to live with her, and her new husband and his teenage years were marked by a very fractious relationship with his stepfather.

Over the years he became more band more withdrawn, and at the age of 24 he severed contact with his family, but and after a series of failed relationships met Samantha Stobart in 2004

The one thing that Raoul was desperate to have, was a stable family life. The one thing he didn't have as a child, and he thought he would get one with Stobart but their six year relationship broke down in 2010 when Moat was imprisoned for the assault of a relative.

1st July 2010, 11am her majesty's prison Durham and moat was released mote was released after serving just over two months after 16-week sentence, devastated by his broken relationship with Samantha, combined with time in the prison with time on his hands to think of his he's jealousies were emphasised with feelings of mistrust to fall towards Samantha and were amplified.

Immediately after being granted his freedom he began to meticulously gather supplies for an attack and armed himself with a sawn-off shotgun finish and to make it even more lethal and normal shotgun cartridge would contain amount of ball bearings

on top of the explosive charge motor
removed a portion of those ball bearings
and packed in smaller items of metal in
there I guess his mindset behind that
was to cause maximum damage

CHAPTER SIX

Timeline of events

At 2:40 AM on the 3rd of July, it took just 48 hours after his release for Moat to put his plan into action, gunning down his ex-girlfriend Samantha Stobart and her new partner Christopher Brown on the surface a vengeful attack by jilted lover but deep down a festering resentment remained and Raul Moats bloody spree was just beginning.

He made a call to Northumbria Police, gave his name, and told them calmly "I am coming to get you"

The 3rd of July 2010 Birtley, Tyne and Wear which was watched over by Anthony Gormley's iconic Angel of the North, overnight this small town had become the scene of a violent crime less than 48 hours after being released from prison 37-year-old rail Moat had shot his ex-girlfriend and murdered her new boyfriend, Christopher Brown.

About a week, maybe two before this happened Christopher Brown was sitting drinking tea in my home as he was arranging Karate lessons my kids and me. Seemed like a very nice guy in the hour or so that met. Such a shame

Raul had met Samantha six years earlier
in 2004, he was a 31-year-old Bouncer
working in Newcastle's thriving club
scene,
she was just 16 years old showed fake
ID to get in. He asked the
question if she was underage for the
club and they got chatting and just went
from there.

Raoul was a bodybuilder and he used to wear these cut out vests that showed that everything off he was proud of his muscles and Sam thought he looked great, she was young she was good looking she had a great figure, and he was a lot older than her, he thought all of his birthdays had come at once.

After six turbulent years together, Samantha gave birth to a baby girl making Moat a father once more.

Having also won custody of two daughters from a previous relationship, this was very important to Raoul, this was something that he aspired to, to be a good father.

When he had children from previous relationships to Samantha things didn't work out, they hadn't achieved the perfect family instead difficult fractious relationships with girlfriends, difficult relationships with these children and had an incredibly

difficult relationship with Samantha Stobart. He was a big character and instigator and could appear very intimidating.

Moat admitted to domestic violence in previous relationships specifically with some stuff but that he did that in a way where he portrayed her as being provocative as if Sam made him do it and this is something very common with domestic violence perpetrators there was always Samantha's fault.

Samantha shouldn't agitate he would say, she shouldn't do this so he would hit her, she would disappear to her sisters, and he would come over sweet talk her and she'd go back and then she would be back for a few months

Then they would have an argument with other each, and would lash out and hit her again and she went to her sisters again back in the position to being a victim a victim of emotional abuse whilst he was behind bars Samantha took the opportunity to put a definitive end to her abusive 6-year relationship with Moat fabricating a story that her new partner was a police officer, when Moat shot and killed Chris Brown a point-blank range, he was still of the belief that Chris Brown was a police officer.

CHAPTER SEVEN

Death of an innocent man

Christopher brown wasn't a police officer that was simply something Samantha had used to try and keep more away, he was a karate instructor, and he was delivering leaflets around the doors when she met him it just seemed like a normal lad who was trying to make a go of things and his only mistake, if you can call it that was, he started to relationship with Samantha.

By telling him her new boyfriend was a police officer Sam really did think that it would persuade Raoul to keep his distance, but she could have picked a worse profession in the world.

Moat had a long running hatred and paranoia about the police, and this was yet another way in which he thought the police had taken something away from them, Moat had a history of dealings with Northumbria Police the vendetta he thought that Northumbria Police had something against him that stretched back many years largely based on minor incidents. The police were always pulling him over the slightest thing, and he was just sick of it, he would often complain that every time he pulled into a petrol station that the police were always there waiting for him, there is the stop him he felt it was non-stop harassment. He was always on edge; he became very paranoid his house had CCTV cameras around eight and recorded all his phone calls with social services and with the police.

He blamed them for his business going bust, he blamed them for constantly harassing him. There must have some reason he would say, "I've never done anything to
promote this" this was his default setting when something didn't go

right in his life, he blamed the police

and he only had one route left to take in

his eyes which was to take revenge

CHAPTER EIGHT

Declaration of war

Twenty-nine minutes past Midnight, July the 4th less than 24 hours after the shootings in Birtley Moat made a chilling phone call to the communication centre at Northumbria Police headquarters.

"Hello this is the gunman from Birtley last night my name is Raul Moat, and I am phoning to tell you exactly why you've

done what I've done right now my girlfriend has been having an affair behind my back with one of your officers this

gentleman that I shot last night, and you police have taken too much off me over the years Police officers over the years I am coming to get you I'm not on the run I'm coming to get you I've lost everything through

you right, you won't leave me alone right, so I am hunting for officers now"

Raoul effectively was making full admissions to shooting Christopher Brown Samantha but more worryingly he is declaring war on Northumbria Police officers Earlier that evening traffic officer PC David Rathband was starting his late shift with the Northumbria Police, under heightened alert for the gunmen from the previous night. David was a very proactive police officer.

Moments after Moats call to the police PC Rathband was sitting in his patrol car unaware that his life was about to be turned upside down.

He had decided to sit up on the A1 one at one of his favourites stopping points on the A1 on the western side of the city of Newcastle near to Denton.

He sits up somewhere like this often where it's very busy with a high volume of traffic coming past and waiting, that's what it all comes down to playing the waiting game. There may be that opportunity for that vehicle, that one vehicle you're looking for come past. Unfortunately for Rathband that night it did.

PC Rathband was unaware Moat had by now changed vehicles changed and was now travelling in a black Lexus. the vehicle he was expecting or hoping to see had had been dumped earlier on that day, but that intelligence hadn't got out yet and so David was effectively sat there waiting to look for something that wasn't going to come past the individual he was looking for did but the car didn't.

That's when it all went horribly wrong just moments after making his call to the Police to declare war Moat, that threat to the police became a brutal reality.

As it transpires Moat drives past and sees David sat in his police car on his own and decided to
stop just on the on slip for the motorway, he got out and carrying her sawn-off shotgun he
crept up to a mount an attack on PC Rathband, who was aware that

somebody was doing something next to his car, he turned looked and saw this large man holding a gun pointed at him through the passenger window PC Rathbands last thought before he was shot was, Oh no it's Raoul Moat and for that split second.

David had been horrifically injured he'd been shot twice in the face, he was left blind there and then, it's not the done thing
to shoot a police officer, for many
there is a line that people don't cross.

For somebody to actively go out and hunt a police officer is almost unheard of, as his third victim fighting for his life.

Raoul Moat disappeared into the night amidst fears that his spree was far from over there was a real sense of concern.

CHAPTER NINE

Hunting the Police

PC Rathband wasn't going to be the final victim, minutes later an agitated mode called Northumbria Police once more it was Moat making it very clear that he was responsible for shooting David Rathband and again emphasise and that he would be hunting more police officers the gunman's behaviour was becoming increasingly irrational

Being his third victim fighting for his life Raoul mode disappeared into the night amidst fears that his spree was far from over there was a real sense of concern that PC Rathband wasn't going to be the final victim minutes later an agitated Moat cold call to Northumbria Police,

"I've just downed your officer at the roundabout in the west end of Newcastle I'm absolutely not going to stop, you're going to have to kill me, I'm never going to stop"

Northumbria Police called an emergency press conference to reach out to Moat. At the press conference the following was read out:

"You have told us that the police are not taking you seriously, I can assure you we are. All I want you to know that you have our full attention" the press conference started, "Innocent people have been
hurt this must stop now with one dead two in a critical condition"

Northumbria police went on to say that

"With clear intent to kill again the elusive Moat needed to be caught before his killing spree claimed further victims"

But with no idea where he was, who he was with in fact no idea where he was hiding out and every inquiry that was made that was an attempt to secure his arrest drew blanks.

They decided to involve specialist firearms officers as this was now a there was a major manhunt then, this was like nothing any of us had ever seen before, and none of the police had ever experienced anything like this before in their careers.

In an unexpected twist that emerged the ruthless spree threatened to escalate further later Sunday afternoon when two separate reports came in which suggested that he may have had hostages.

The reports coming from the family of Karl Ness and the family of Qhuram Awan

As is typical in a hostage situation the police request to the media that they don't report that information because it may affect the safe recovery of the hostages.

They were now aware that Moat was travelling in a black Lexus, it had distinctive engine noise and an appeal was put out to the public to help find that car.

Very quickly it was identified being moved from the Tyne and Wear area to the rural countryside of Northumberland to Rothbury

The search moved into a new area and with the lives of two hostages in his hands the need to find Moat, it took on a new urgency worried that was potentially spiralling out of control.

CHAPTER TEN

Rothbury, Northumberland

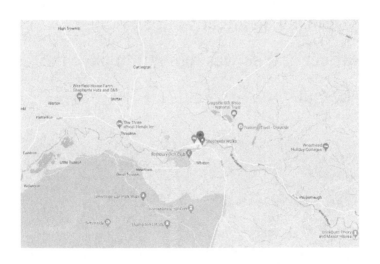

As the manhunt moved to a new area and with the lives of two hostages in his hands the need to find Moat took on a new urgency his savage spree was potentially spiralling out of control this man threatened to kill police officers this man had already shot a police officer and he was thought to have the shotgun

RHY 43   General View, Rothbury.

This small market town sits in the rolling hills of Northumberland if you drive north from Newcastle you come to Rothbury, it's a nice place somewhere I had spent happy days with family growing up, it's everyone's idea a quaint little village in the hills.

A quite place where everybody knows everybody else and a small close-knit community, but Rothbury was about to become the focus of the world's attention,

until the first police car drove up the street it was just an ordinary day.

As the hunt for the gunman and his hostages intensified police resources poured into the immediate area, the manhunt would soon reach unprecedented levels involving over 500 officers and a two-mile exclusion zone was set up in the Rothbury area.

As this unfolded, I was 20 miles away, camping with my family in the small Northumberland town of Wooler, even there it was all anyone was talking about, and it inspired fear in many people on that campsite.

It was clear that any arrest of Moat was going to involve the use of armed police officers, there is no other way to do it. The police were on high alert for

a potential hostage stand-off but the story was about to take an unexpected turn Moat had already revealed that he had taken some hostages, but it became apparent that the police were unsure as to whether they were hostages or accomplices were in cahoots with Moat.

Karl Ness and Qhuram Awan one was

in fact in collusion with the gunman,

Moat

CHAPTER ELEVEN

COLLUSION

Both men with Moat had each delivered two messages to their families, one appeared to be a genuine hostage letter but the second was a note explaining that they were actually in the safe hands of their friend Raul Moat and to burn the second letter. Their concerned families both submitted these letters to the police, who were quickly trying more resource moved.

Moat during this time was able to melt into the countryside, whereas the so-called hostages try to make their escape along the open road.

The police helicopter was very quickly above them, one police car drove past them with an officer into identify them once he did that he radios to colleagues

who followed in a second police car who drove up to them fast in unmarked cars and threw

thunder flash's out their feet this momentarily stunned and other officers came out and arrested them at gunpoint with them both in custody the full extent of their involvement in Moats rampage, they were both friends of Moat especially Karl Ness.

They had driven Raoul to Samantha Stobart's house so there's no doubt that they were fully involved. CCTV footage then emerged that revealed the movements of Moat and his accomplices before and during his spree there caught on Camera

buying him things from Tesco it seemed almost like they were

getting ready for an s even adventure.

They were buying barbecue sauce and all sorts of everyday items too, including camping gear, but what led two men to assist Raul Moat in his vengeful rampage?

Moat was known to be highly manipulative; he was able to make people feel as if they were in the wrong as if they'd wronged him and that gave him leverage to get to get other people to do what he wanted them to do.

They were very strange characters in this in this because they didn't seem to gain anything other than in away looking up to Moat, they wanted to impress him they were more than willing to help them carry out these horrific acts and there was nothing in it for them.

Karl Ness a bodybuilder and former nightclub doorman had known Moat for several years having also worked as a bouncer in Newcastle.

During Moats incarceration he had been in regular contact with Moat, through prison visits and telephone calls but one conversation was really interesting in that he asked Ness to get a particular individual to visit him while he was in prison because he was an individual who could get him what he described was a car with six wheels and the police looked at the people involved my only explanation for a car with 60 uses a gun and the associated ammunition.

CHAPTER TWELVE

Closing In

The 7th of July 2010 Rothbury Northumberland the day following the arrests of a one and less with mode still at large police discovered a makeshift campsite where he had been hiding out amongst the debris a disturbing message from Moat was found forcing the police to take urgent action police called us all in further an emergency press

conference and told us that they

had found a Dictaphone that the motor left in one of the places that had been camping out on that he gives details of the fact that he's been following the media coverage that

you've been angered by it he was getting very very agitated by the way who's been portrayed in the price, and he decided that, or he declared on that Dictaphone that for every lie it was told he would shoot innocent member of the public information has now emerged that Mr Moat has made

=threats towards the wider public

fearing for public safety a media

blackout was imposed police told us about this threat and request to not publish the material that might upset Moat when they explained the reason why there was a collective draining of colour from faces because none of us

wanted to put anyone at any further risk than they already

were on the 8th of July 2 days after the arrest of Ness and A1 and mote was still on the run, he no longer had a car he no longer had access to money or as far as anyone knew no longer access to the outside world he wasn't in touch with anybody else so his ability to move around had clearly been reduced but how was this former nightclub bouncer evading capture in the Northumbrian wilderness we knew he had a love of Rothbury, and he was frequently in in Rothbury enjoyed camping it was an area that was familiar to him. The Police actually spoke to an ex-girlfriend of his who lived in the village, he also used to go fishing there he knew the area, so he knew what he was doing.

You always feel more comfortable in an environment that you're familiar with, you know you can relax and soon take stock and make a plan from there.

Despite the two-mile exclusion zone setup by the police and challenging terrain is plenty of opportunities to remain invisible it's quite rugged terrain there's lots of farms there's lots of fields there's probably lots of places that you could hideout that a lot of people wouldn't know about if you look at the amount of forest round here that's agreed please to

be straight away because the helicopter can't see you.

CHAPTER THIRTEEN

Living in Fear

The police search continued with no reported sightings of Moat tension in the Rothbury area was rising people were scared everyone was conscious that there was an armed and dangerous man on the loose rumours were rife knowing that the gunmen could even be living amongst them.

There were rumours around might had gone into the centre of the village during the manhunt just over here is the storm drain where it's thought that row was hiding out people were

saying that there are storm drains that lead underneath the village that you could go from remote area and actually end up coming up through a drain in the village so you can nip in in the early hours of the morning and

just become a Scotland Jack scavenging and in the bins in

allotments greenhouses these are the gardens behind the wall where it's thought that Robert was going into steel vegetables and food like the guy at the bottom of the village who found his tomatoes, we're going missing I mean there were different scientists are in different places there was a house that he potentially went into and lay down on the bed because residents had reported like an imprint of his head in the pillow.

As Moat continued to remain one step ahead of the police local residents were becoming increasingly unnerved, but I think there is a little moment of panic because obviously when the police add telling you to get him locked the doors stay away from the windows, you're assuming this is going to be bullet flying all over the place no one quite knew how much ammunition or how many guns he had in his possession.

There was a real sense of fear throughout the area when public safety's your priority the police

had saturated Rothbury so that in

the event of any siting or any confrontation.

CHAPTER FOURTEEN

Found!

At 7:25 PM on the 9th of July, six days after the vengeful rampage began a member of the public reported sighting a man answering Moats description on the banks of the river near the centre of Rothbury.

As armed police descended, a stand-off developed and when Moat saw them, he slowly raised the shotgun, the very same gun that he had used on Samantha

Stobart, Christopher Brown and PC David Rathband, as it slowly raised it became apparent that he wasn't pointing at the police, he pointed it to his own head.

Was his intention that it would end in that field in Rothbury tonight? It certainly looked that way.

Moat had embarked on a vengeful killing spree leaving one dead and two critically wounded, it was starting to look like he would evade justice.

He was now at Rothbury Riverside having evaded capture for further three days, now finally cornered in an area on the edge of the river with nowhere else to go.

The press centre and public were immediately cleared from the area

CHAPTER FIFTEEN

GAZZA

Paul Gascoigne's bizarre bid to 'save' killer Raoul Moat after 14 lines of cocaine

Former England international Gazza was convinced he was Raoul Moat's brother and arrived at a police stand-off in his dressing gown with chicken, lager and a fishing rod

In what can only be seen as a bizarre twist of fate a night in shining armour rode into town to save the day, well that's what he thought anyway. A battered Ford Mondeo was his steed and the sword had been swapped for a fishing rod, a chicken and a can of larger.

Former professional footballer Paul Gascoigne aka Gazza who hailed from the town of Dunstan, Gateshead at the south side of the River Tyne, in god's country not too far from Moat.

Staggering out of the taxi worse for the wear as usual after drinking heavily and sniffing Columbian marching powder no doubt faster than Henry the Hoover, calling out *"Moaty, Moaty it's me Gazza where are you mate"*

He was convinced he was Raoul Moat's brother when he arrived at the police stand-off in his dressing gown with chicken, lager and a fishing rod
While Moat stood with a sawn-off shot gun aimed at his neck, former England international turned up to the tense stand-off. He even spoke to a radio phone in show live.

He called into the Real Radio show when arriving saying, *"I did not phone up for a publicity stunt right OK, just the public and I am I'm sitting there was bored nothing do it came on telly, he has been a good friend of mine and then I decided I was getting him a jacket, and food and I am staying in a bed*

and breakfast up the road cause I've done the taxi yeah I am sure I could stay there and then I was gonna walk through the mountains I know all the rivers roughly I know everywhere in Rothbury and I was gonna walkthrough the hills and shout out his name or just going to put some chicken some bread down I know it's important Moaty I will message you went out looking for him I've got a Newcastle United jacket for him on top of what I've got him and I was going to go through the Moors on my own in a pitch keep shouting his name because I know he wouldn't shoot me, I know

I'm a good friend to him and I am shouting Moaty's its Gaza I know it's something wrong has been given drugs, without anyone he will listen to me I am concerned the guy is a nice guy like that yeah I would let him order me just meet him but if he goes to jail I'll going to go to gaol I will visit him a couple of times a month but I do want him to say to any stranger all I wanna do is speak of him and I guarantee I think I'm really the guy, that he would talk to him"

CHAPTER SIXTEEN

THE END IS NEIGH

The final hours of Raoul Moats life were played out on the riverbank, as the standoff between police and Raoul unfolded the nation was captivated by rolling 24-hour news. It was a waiting game during the final hours between Moat and the police.

It was live on every news channel and as journalists at the newspaper were watching and waiting, glued to the television at night and waiting for things to happen the whole world looked on transfixed on what was happening in Rothbury

The whole process of getting him to surrender the police thought was happening but it went on, all the time the former Newcastle Bouncer lay on the bank, gun underneath his neck.

Armed officers and negotiators were there for the long haul, behind the scenes police have been analysing Moats behaviour throughout this pre preparing for every eventuality because Moat had made contact with Northumbria Police a couple of times and telephone there was always a likelihood that he may call back again.

He got annoyed when they spoke to him emotionally about close relationships, he was immune to any

requests that they made of him stop or persuade him that he should surrender but after six hours of negotiation the mood of the stalemate changed as Moat became increasingly agitated.

The Police couldn't really see what was happening, but you could hear that there was a commotion at that point it was clear to everybody present that he had made his mind up he was ready to finish the whole episode.

Just then the police attempted to incapacitate Moat with a shotgun style tsar

There were a couple of sounds which clearly sounded like gunshots in the night air, at 1.15 am almost immediately after the police tzars were discharged Raoul Moat fired the final shot of his killing spree, but this time the indented target was himself.

An ambulance crew took him to Newcastle General Hospital and shortly after his arrival he was pronounced dead.

CHAPTER SEVENTEEN

THE DAYS FOLLOWING

The week after the biggest British manhunt of a generation involving over 500 police officers and costing Northumbria Police in excess of £1,000,000.

Raoul Moats ruthless rampage was finally over. For him it seemed that it Had come to a point where he didn't want to live, there was nothing and nobody left for him and when you get that point, when you start feeling like that then there's really only one

way it's going to end, and he had

actually said this to the negotiators. It

was his attention that it would end the

way

CHAPTER EIGHTEEN

PC David Rathband

It seemed that David Rathband kept hitting the headlines in subsequent years but for all thew wrong reasons, including domestic violence arrest after assaulting his wife, and affair with a 7/7 survivor and then ultimately his death after talking his own life in 2012.

August 2011 (Credit: Newcastle Evening Chronicle)

PC David Rathband arrested over assault

RAOUL Moat victim David Rathband has been arrested on suspicion of assault; police have confirmed.

Inquiries are ongoing into the incident which saw the blinded PC detained at his home in Cramlington, Northumberland, late on Tuesday night.

The 43-year-old, gunned down and blinded by on-the-run killer Raoul Moat last year, was arrested just before midnight on Tuesday, but released a short time later.

It is not known if any guests were at the family home, he shares with his wife Kath and two teenage children.

A spokeswoman for the police officer denied he had been involved in an assault of any kind. She said: "We have no comment to make regarding this alleged arrest other than no allegations were made or are being made by any person concerning David Rathband's conduct.

"The family are understandably still coming to terms with the huge impact and changes to their lives as a result of the serious injuries sustained by David whilst on duty and they therefore request that their privacy is respected during this difficult time."

A spokeswoman for Northumbria Police said: "At 11.51pm on Tuesday, August 23, police were called to a report of an assault at a residential address in Lyndale, Cramlington.

"Officers attended and a 43-year-old man was arrested on suspicion of assault. Inquiries are ongoing."

A Tweet posted the day after the arrest hinted at the shooting victim's on-going struggle to come to terms with the disability the attack has left him with.

The blinded bobby re-tweeted a message from Empire Your Life Today, which read: ***The more anger towards the past you carry in your heart, the*** *less capable you are of loving in the present. ~ Barbara De Angelis."*

Ahead of the incident which led to Rathband's arrest, he re-tweeted a message from his twin brother Darren Rathband, which said: "Some people just make it even harder. Fools come in all shapes."

Tweets from earlier in the week suggested the dad-of-two had been struggling to sleep.

On Monday night he wrote: "Alcohol next sleeping pills not working." On Saturday, the officer Tweeted: "Lots on my mind."

PC Rathband also used his Twitter profile to reveal he had attended hospital on Tuesday morning to have metal pellets removed from his face.

X-rays show the blinded officer was left with hundreds of shards of metal in his face and scalp after he was shot at close range by Moat.

The PC thanked medics at Newcastle's Royal Victoria Infirmary by posting: "Thanks to staff 21 RVI Mr D Max consultant and his team my hero's."

Family's concern for hero PC David Rathband following wife assault arrest (Credit: Daily Record, Scotland)

The officer, 43, blinded by gunman Raoul Moat last year, was quizzed by police at his home over the alleged attack on wife Kath, 41.

The sister of hero PC David Rathband spoke of her concern for him yesterday following his arrest for an alleged assault on his wife.

The officer, 43, blinded by gunman Raoul Moat last year, was quizzed by police at his home in Cramlington, Northumberland, last Tuesday over the alleged attack on wife Kath, 41.

Debbie Essery said: "This is all very upsetting, and it has been a stressful time. David is not a well man.

Obviously, I am not going to speak about what happened, but we are all distressed."

Pc Rathband's parents Marilyn, 67, and Keith, 69, have not spoken to him for years. His sisters Karen and Julie have remained loyal to their parents, while twin brother Darren and Debbie have stood by him.

(Credit: The Guardian)

Pc David Rathband: Estranged wife 'could not forgive officer left blind by gunman Raoul Moat over affair with 7/7 survivor Lisa French'

A police officer blinded by gunman Raoul Moat in 2010 began an affair with a survivor from the 7/7 London bombings, an inquest into his death heard today.

Mr Rathband, a 44-year-old father of two, was found hanging at his home in Blyth in Northumberland in February 2012.

CHAPTER EIGHTEEN

I AM SO SO SORRY

In 2020 one of moats children spoke out to the press, saying she was sickened knowing she was his "flesh and blood".

Katelaine has spoken publicly about her dad for the first time in ten years now

21 and living near Newcastle, has decided to speak up after nearly a decade.

She was quoted to say *"I'm so sorry to the people he has hurt. If I had the chance to meet the victims and their families and say I'm so sorry for what my dad did, and show that I care, I would."*

Katelaine added: *"Being his flesh and blood sickens me at times, it's hard to believe who I am.*

"I can't believe I come from that man.

"I'm so glad I didn't know him, and that I became the person I am today despite all I have been through."

While at school Katelaine said she was relentlessly bullied, getting taunted by her fellow pupils due to her physical similarity to her biological father.

She admitted with frank honesty that she still yearns for the dad she never knew and writes him a birthday card every year on June 17 – but added she then burns it and releases a balloon to float away.

Katelaine said: *"It is not about honouring him. It is not for him, but for me, for my peace of mind.*

"I do a little speech in my head. One year it might be: 'I hope you're proud of me despite everything you have done.' Other times I have thought: 'Why couldn't you just be the right person? Do the right thing?'"

She also told of how she had been using a social media app recently which swapped the sex of people in pictures.

She described the result as horrifying, adding she regretted it and when she showed her mum, she "nearly had a heart attack" as she looked just like an 18-year-old Raoul Moat.

When Katelaine was young she thought the ex-partner of her mum Caroline was her dad, until a relative revealed the truth when she was around seven.

Mum Caroline had wanted to protect her young daughter from the shocking truth. Katelaine later learnt Moat had attacked her mum a number of times after the pair met in 1996.

When Caroline told him she was pregnant he threatened to kill the unborn child that would become Katelaine.

Caroline later took out an injunction against Moat and he refused to ever meet the little girl. They learnt the horrors Moat had inflicted from a TV report.

Under police protection they went to stay with relatives in the Midlands.

Although Katelaine now suffers from depression she is settled and in a happy relationship and hopes to become a career.

She has also managed to build up a relationship in the past four years with two of Moat's other children.

CCHAPTEWR NINETEEN

Sue Sim

In July 2010, Sue Sim, Temporary Chief Constable of Northumbria Police, received a call in the middle of the night to say there had been a double shooting in a quiet suburb near Newcastle. The cat-and-mouse search for the gunman Raoul Moat involved specialist police units, snipers, RAF jets and played out live to a worldwide TV audience.

In an interview in 2021 for Sky News, Sue said

"On 3rd July 2010 I was in overall command of Northumbria Force, I was at home I'd gone to bed as normal my eldest daughter and

]husband were in bed and then I received that fateful call.

It was in the early hours of the morning that police were called to this normally quiet area of Birtley".

"It was the Silver Commander who phoned me to say that there had been a shooting and that they

arrived to find a scene of brutal violence."

"I lived in Newcastle and just across the river time the next metropolitan district was Gateshead, and it was in that area that the shootings took place"

"The former boyfriend of Samantha Stobart had in a fit of jealousy shot and murdered Chris Brown and seriously injured Samantha"

"I thought at that point that what we had to do then was just to locate Raoul Moat I did not in

anyway, shape or form expect it to turn into the incident that it did"

"Moat put a call in to us at Northumbria Police to say that he was going to shoot police officers"

"He had promised not to stop until he was dead. When I got a phone call, which was the worst phone call of my professional life to say he shot through a police car window into the face of an officer"

"PC David Rathband was sitting waiting and hoping too actually

stop Moat stop at the roundabout on the A1 and A 69 junction, Moat had gone up to him and had callously shot him in the head which resulted in David being blinded"

"I gave a press statement to say we are absolutely committed to finding the man who did this and are using every resource available to bring this to a conclusion as quickly as possible"

"Nobody really knew what this man was going to do next we had a gun man on the run"

"My greatest fear was not being able to bring him to justice and my first objective was to make sure that he was detained and brought to justice before a court for his crimes and that was the one thing that I wanted as well as keeping the community and the police officers safe"

"We knew that he had gone to ground in Rothbury what I was concerned about was the fact that we were unable to locate him. Rothbury is in Northumberland and where Moat was is one of the most densely wooded and least

Populated parts of Northumberland"

"We were almost assembling a small army in the most unlikely of places there were reinforcements coming in from all over the country 250 of them were armed and we set up a two-mile exclusion zone with roadblocks everywhere you couldn't get in or out of that town without your car been searched"

"We also had RAF Tornado Jets flying quite slowly over Rothbury they were being used to

photograph and video the terrain to try and spot any sign of where he had been"

"I think the thing that did cause me some angst was that some of my male chief constable colleagues had decided but I didn't have the experience because I was only a temporary chief constable. I had a call from then home secretary Terresa May and her advisors found me on a daily basis"

"A community officer had walked down by the riverbank and

had actually seen him and had called the firearms in to surround him and to start negotiating with him, I wasn't aware of that at that time I had left Rothbury just after six o'clock and after we got down to the A1 the assistant chief

constable called me and said sue, we've got him surrounded on the riverbank"

"This was the moment everything had been building towards some officers were taking cover behind armoured vehicles there were snipers with rifles some of them were literally standing in the

river using anywhere to try and get a sight of Moat, we thought that Moat was going to kill again, and we were throwing everything at it to try and stop him"

"I went to headquarters into the gold command and I stayed there my sole objective was to capture Raoul Moat and put him before a court, all of a sudden the call came, shots fired, I was asking who shot who, shot and it became clear very very quickly the Moat had shot himself and the ambulance was down there and took him to the hospital where he was declared dead"

"I have to live with the fact we couldn't bring him to justice for the families of the people that he hurt, and I would like to give, as I did at the time, my condolences to the family of Chris Brown to

Kath Rathband and the children of David Rathband for his terrible death following this incident, and for Samantha Stobart for the injuries that she had they were also the innocent victims of this man "

Credit: Sky News Storycast

Printed in Great Britain
by Amazon

37886694R00076